Affiliate Marketing on

YouTube:

Tips and Techniques for Creating Video Content That Promotes Affiliate Products and Generates Revenue

Affiliate Marketing

Automation:

Using Tools and Software to Automate Various Aspects of the Affiliate Marketing Process, Such As Tracking, Reporting, and Payment Processing

High-Ticket Affiliate

Marketing:

Strategies for promoting high-value products and services and earning large commissions.

The Complete 3 in 1 Affiliate Marketing Book

Mellisa G Norton

Table of Content

About The Author

Mellisa G Norton is an avid writer, teacher, top-notch content writer in diverse areas of life.

The author is an expert and thought leader in the field of affiliate marketing who have written many books, created online courses, and shared his knowledge through blogs and podcasts.

I have helped thousands of people achieve success in the affiliate marketing industry and have shared my expertise through a variety of media.

If you're interested in learning more about affiliate marketing, high ticket affiliate marketing, and affiliate marketing automation, consider exploring the facts and figures presented in this book. With the right knowledge and strategies, you too can achieve financial freedom and build a successful business through affiliate marketing.

Description

Are you to take your YouTube channel to the next level and start earning big bucks? Look no further than the power of affiliate marketing!

With traditional affiliate marketing, you can earn a commission by promoting a variety of products and services to your audience. But if you're looking to make serious money, high ticket affiliate marketing is where it's at. By promoting high-priced items like luxury goods, high-end electronics, and exclusive coaching programs, you can earn commissions of thousands of dollars per sale.

And to really optimize your earnings, you'll want to consider affiliate marketing automation. By streamlining the affiliate marketing process with software and tools, you can save time and effort while also maximizing your profits. From tracking affiliate links to managing commissions and monitoring performance metrics, automation is the key to success in the competitive world of affiliate marketing.

But don't my words for it. Many successful YouTubers have used the power of affiliate marketing, high ticketing marketing, and automation to build thriving businesses and generate substantial income streams. And with the vast audience and reach of the YouTube, the potential for success is practically limitless.

So what are waiting for? In this book, you will see reputable affiliate programs, sign up today and start promoting products and services to your engaged audience. With the right strategies and tools, you can achieve financial freedom and live the life of your dreams.

Affiliate Marketing on YouTube:

Tips and Techniques for Creating Video Content That Promotes Affiliate Products and Generates Revenue

Chapter 1

Introduction

Affiliate marketing on YouTube has become an increasingly popular way for content creators to monetize their channels and earn income through commissions on sales. By promoting products and services that align with their niche and audience, YouTubers can earn commissions on sales generated through their unique affiliate links. However, affiliate marketing on YouTube requires more than just adding links to video descriptions. It involves developing a content strategy that integrates affiliate marketing in a way that feels natural and provides value to viewers.

In this book, we'll provide a comprehensive guide to affiliate marketing on YouTube, including everything from setting up your channel for success to finding the right products to promote, creating content that converts, growing your audience and brand, and analyzing and optimizing your results. We'll also cover advanced techniques for scaling your affiliate marketing efforts and maximizing your commissions.

Whether you're a seasoned YouTuber looking to monetize your content or a newcomer looking to start a channel and earn income through affiliate

marketing, this book will provide you with the knowledge and strategies you need to succeed. So let's dive in and explore the exciting world of affiliate marketing on YouTube!

1.1 Definition of affiliate marketing on YouTube

Affiliate marketing on YouTube is a monetization strategy that involves content creators promoting products or services to their audience and earning commissions on sales generated through unique affiliate links. YouTubers partner with brands and companies to promote their products or services through sponsored videos, product reviews, tutorials, and other types of content that align with their niche and audience. When viewers click on the affiliate links provided in the video description and make a purchase, the content creator earns a commission on that sale. This is a win-win for both the YouTuber and the brand, as the YouTuber earns income through commissions and the brand gains exposure and potential sales through the YouTuber's audience.

1.2 Benefits of affiliate marketing on YouTube

Affiliate marketing on YouTube offers several benefits for content creators looking to monetize their channels:

- **Passive Income**: Affiliate marketing allows YouTubers to earn passive income through commissions on sales generated through their unique affiliate links. This means they can continue to earn income from their videos long after they have been published.

- **Monetization Flexibility**: Affiliate marketing offers monetization flexibility for YouTubers, as they can choose products and services to promote that align with their niche and audience. They can also choose how they want to promote the products, whether it's through product reviews, tutorials, or other types of content.

- **Cost-effective**: Affiliate marketing is a cost-effective way for brands to promote their products, as they only pay commissions on sales generated through the YouTuber's unique affiliate link. This means they don't have to pay upfront for advertising or other marketing costs.

- **Audience Trust**: Affiliate marketing on YouTube allows YouTubers to build trust with their audience by promoting products and services that they personally use and recommend.

This can lead to higher conversion rates and increased sales for the brands they promote.

- **Brand Awareness**: Affiliate marketing on YouTube can help brands gain exposure to new audiences and increase brand awareness. This can be especially effective for new or niche brands looking to gain traction in their industry.

Overall, affiliate marketing on YouTube can be a lucrative and effective way for content creators to monetize their channels while providing value to their audience and promoting products and services they believe in.

Chapter 2

Setting Up Your YouTube Channel

2.1 Creating a YouTube channel

Creating a YouTube channel is an essential step for anyone who wants to succeed on the platform. As someone who has gone through the process myself, I can confidently say that creating a YouTube channel is relatively easy and straightforward.

The first step is to create a Google account if you don't already have one. Then, go to YouTube.com and sign in with your Google account. Once you're signed in, click on your profile picture in the top right corner and select "Create a channel." You'll be prompted to choose a channel name and category.

One important thing to keep in mind when creating a YouTube channel is to choose a name that reflects your niche and content. This will help viewers understand what your channel is about and make it easier for them to find you. Additionally, make sure to fill out your channel description and add an eye-catching profile picture and banner to make your channel look professional and appealing.

After you've created your channel, it's time to start creating content. Before you start filming, take some time to research your niche and audience and plan out your content strategy. This will help you create videos that are engaging and valuable to your viewers.

Here's a detailed breakdown of the steps involved in creating a YouTube channel:

Step 1: Create a Google account

To create a YouTube channel, you first need to create a Google account if you don't already have one. You can do this by going to the Google homepage and clicking on the "Sign in" button in the top right corner. If you don't have an account, click on the "Create account" link and follow the instructions to set up a new account.

Step 2: Go to YouTube.com

Once you have a Google account, go to YouTube.com and sign in with your Google account credentials. If you're already signed in to your Google account, click on your profile picture in the top right corner of the screen and select "YouTube" from the dropdown menu.

Step 3: Create a channel

To create a channel, click on your profile picture in the top right corner of the screen and select "Create a channel" from the dropdown menu. You'll be prompted to choose a name for your channel, as well as a category that best describes the type of content you'll be creating.

Step 4: Customize your channel

After you've created your channel, it's time to customize it to make it look appealing and professional. Start by adding a profile picture and banner image that reflects your brand and content. You can also add a channel description to give viewers an idea of what your channel is all about.

Step 5: Plan your content strategy

Before you start creating videos, it's important to plan your content strategy. This involves researching your niche and audience, identifying the types of videos that are popular in your niche, and planning out your content calendar.

Step 6: Create and upload videos

Once you have a plan in place, it's time to start creating videos. You can film your videos using a smartphone or a camera, and edit them using video editing software like Adobe Premiere Pro or iMovie. Once your video is ready, you can upload it to your channel by clicking on the "Upload" button on your channel homepage.

Overall, creating a YouTube channel is a relatively simple process that requires some planning and attention to detail. By following these steps and putting in the time and effort to create high-quality content, you can build a successful presence on the platform and grow your audience over time.

2.2 Optimizing your channel for affiliate marketing

Optimizing your YouTube channel is critical for success in affiliate marketing. A well-optimized channel can drive traffic to your affiliate products, increase your visibility, and boost your earnings. Here are some key factors to consider when optimizing your channel for affiliate marketing:

- **Branding**: Your channel branding is the first thing that visitors see, so it's important to make a good impression. Make sure that your channel banner, profile picture, and thumbnails are high-quality, visually appealing, and consistent with your brand.

- **Content**: Your content is the heart of your channel, so it's important to create high-quality, engaging content that resonates with your target audience. Consider the products or services you want to promote as an affiliate and create content that aligns with those offers. This can include product reviews, tutorials, or demonstrations.

- **Keywords**: YouTube is a search engine, so incorporating relevant keywords into your video titles, descriptions, and tags is crucial for optimizing your channel for search. Use tools like Google Keyword Planner or TubeBuddy to find relevant keywords to include in your content.

- **Call-to-action**: Don't forget to include a call-to-action in your videos to encourage viewers to click on your affiliate links. This can be as simple as including a link in your video description or adding an end screen with a clickable button.

- **Engagement**: Engage with your viewers by responding to comments and encouraging them to subscribe to your channel. Building a community of loyal viewers can help boost your channel's visibility and increase your chances of making sales through affiliate marketing.

- **Analytics**: Use YouTube's analytics tools to track your channel's performance, including views, watch time, and engagement. This information can help you identify which videos are performing well and adjust your content strategy accordingly.

Optimizing your YouTube channel for affiliate marketing takes time and effort, but it can pay off in the form of increased traffic, visibility, and earnings. By focusing on branding, content, keywords, call-to-action, engagement, and analytics, you can create a well-optimized channel that attracts viewers and drives sales through affiliate marketing.

2.3 Developing your niche and content strategy

One of the most important factors in succeeding with affiliate marketing on YouTube is developing a niche and content strategy that resonates with your audience. Here are some tips to help you get started:

- **Identify your niche**: Your niche is the specific topic or theme that your channel will revolve around. It's important to choose a niche that you are passionate about and have expertise in. This will allow you to create high-quality content that resonates with your audience and establishes you as an authority in your field.

- **Conduct keyword research**: Once you have identified your niche, it's important to conduct keyword research to identify the specific topics and keywords that your audience is searching for. This will help you to create content that is optimized for search engines and will attract viewers who are interested in your niche.

- **Develop your content strategy**: Based on your niche and keyword research, you can develop a content strategy that outlines the types of videos you will create, the topics you will cover, and the frequency of your uploads. It's important to create a mix of content that includes informative videos, product reviews, and promotional content.

- **Focus on providing value**: Your content should focus on providing value to your viewers. This means creating videos that are informative, entertaining, and engaging. You should also focus on building a relationship with your audience by responding to comments and engaging with your viewers.

- **Optimize your videos for search engines**: To attract more viewers to your channel, it's important to optimize your videos for search engines. This includes using relevant keywords in your video titles, descriptions, and tags, and creating high-quality content that is engaging and informative.

By following these tips, you can develop a niche and content strategy that will help you to succeed with affiliate marketing on YouTube. Remember, the key to success is creating high-quality content that provides value to your audience and establishes you as an authority in your field.

Chapter 3

Finding Affiliate Products to Promote

3.1 Identifying affiliate programs and networks

Identifying affiliate programs and networks is an essential step in affiliate marketing on YouTube.

It involves finding products or services that align with your niche and that you can promote to your audience through your content. Here are some steps to help you identify the right affiliate programs and networks for your channel:

- **Research your niche**: Before you can start looking for affiliate programs, you need to have a clear understanding of your niche and the products or services that your audience is interested in. Conduct research on your niche and identify popular products or services that are relevant to your content.

- **Check for affiliate programs**: Once you have a list of products or services that you want to promote, check if there are affiliate programs for them. You can do this by visiting the websites of the products or services and looking for information on their affiliate programs. Alternatively, you can use affiliate program directories like ClickBank, Commission Junction, or ShareASale to search for relevant affiliate programs.

- **Check for affiliate networks**: Affiliate networks are platforms that connect affiliates with multiple affiliate programs. They offer a wide range of products and services that you can promote, making it easier to find relevant offers for your niche. Some popular affiliate networks include Amazon Associates, Rakuten Marketing, and CJ Affiliate.

- **Evaluate affiliate programs and networks**: Once you have identified potential affiliate programs and networks, evaluate them based on factors like commission rates, payment schedules, tracking and reporting tools, and support for affiliates. Choose programs and networks that offer competitive commission rates, reliable tracking and reporting, and good support for affiliates.

- **Apply for affiliate programs**: After identifying suitable affiliate programs and networks, you need to apply for them. Follow the application process, which may involve filling out a form or submitting your website or channel for review. Be sure to read the terms and conditions of the programs carefully to ensure that you comply with their guidelines.

By following these steps, you can identify suitable affiliate programs and networks for your YouTube channel and start promoting products or services to your audience. Remember to disclose your affiliate partnerships in your content and to provide value to your audience by promoting products or services that are relevant and useful to them.

3.2 Finding products that align with your niche and audience

When it comes to affiliate marketing on YouTube, finding products that align with your niche and audience is crucial to the success of your channel. You want to promote products that your viewers will be interested in and will be likely to purchase.

One way to find products that align with your niche and audience is to do some research on affiliate programs and networks. There are many affiliate programs and networks available, such as Amazon Associates, ClickBank, and ShareASale, that offer a wide range of products for you to promote.

To start, consider the niche of your channel and the interests of your audience. What types of products would they be interested in purchasing? What problems or needs do they have that can be solved with a product?

Once you have a clear understanding of your audience and their needs, you can search for affiliate programs and networks that offer relevant products. Look for products that are high-quality, offer good commission rates, and have a good reputation.

Another way to find products that align with your niche and audience is to reach out to companies directly. Many companies have their own affiliate programs, and they may be willing to work with you if you have a large following and can promote their products effectively.

When promoting affiliate products, it's important to be transparent with your viewers and let them know that you will receive a commission if they make a purchase through your link. This can help build trust and credibility with your audience, and can ultimately lead to more conversions and sales.

Overall, finding products that align with your niche and audience is an essential part of affiliate marketing on YouTube. By doing your research and choosing high-quality products that your viewers will be interested in, you can increase your chances of success and earn more commissions.

3.3 Evaluating the potential profitability of affiliate products

When it comes to affiliate marketing, evaluating the potential profitability of products is crucial for your success. After all, you want to ensure that the products you promote are not only relevant to your audience but also profitable for you.

Here are some key factors to consider when evaluating the potential profitability of affiliate products:

- **Commission Rates**: The commission rate is the percentage of the sale price that you'll receive as a commission. Look for products with higher commission rates to increase your earnings.

- **Price Point**: The price point of the product is also an important consideration. Look for products that are priced high enough to generate substantial commissions, but not so high that they are unaffordable for your audience.

- **Conversion Rate**: The conversion rate is the percentage of visitors who take the desired action (i.e., make a purchase) after clicking on your affiliate link. Look for products with a high conversion rate to increase your chances of earning a commission.

- **Relevance**: The product you promote should be relevant to your niche and audience. If it's not, you'll have a harder time convincing your audience to make a purchase.

- **Reputation**: You also want to consider the reputation of the product and the company behind it. Promoting products from reputable companies can increase your credibility and trustworthiness with your audience.
- **Demand**: Finally, you want to consider the demand for the product. Look for products that are in high demand to increase your chances of making sales.

By considering these factors, you can evaluate the potential profitability of affiliate products and make informed decisions about which products to promote to your audience. Remember, it's not just about promoting any product – it's about promoting the right products to the right audience at the right time.

Chapter 4

Creating Content That Converts

4.1 Creating videos that promote affiliate products

Creating videos that promote affiliate products is a crucial step in affiliate marketing on YouTube. These videos can include product reviews, tutorials, demonstrations, comparisons, and other types of content that showcase the benefits and features of the affiliate products. Here are some tips for creating effective videos that promote affiliate products:

- **Start with a hook**: Capture your audience's attention from the very beginning of your video with a hook that piques their interest and motivates them to keep watching.

- **Be informative and engaging**: Provide your viewers with valuable information about the affiliate products you're promoting, and make sure to present it in an engaging and entertaining way that keeps them interested.

- **Show, don't tell**: Use visuals and demonstrations to show your viewers the benefits and features of the affiliate products, rather than just telling them about them.

- **Be authentic and honest**: Your viewers trust you, so it's important to be authentic and honest when promoting affiliate products. Be transparent about your relationship with the product and any potential biases you may have.

- **Include a clear call-to-action**: At the end of your video, make sure to include a clear call-to-action that encourages your viewers to click on your affiliate links and make a purchase.

- **Optimize for SEO**: Use relevant keywords and tags in your video's title, description, and tags to help it rank higher in YouTube search results and attract more viewers.

- **Keep it short and sweet**: Attention spans on YouTube are short, so keep your videos concise and to-the-point. Aim for a length of 5-10 minutes for maximum engagement.

By following these tips, you can create videos that effectively promote affiliate products and drive sales, while also providing value to your viewers and building trust with your audience.

4.2 Creating Videos That Promote Affiliate Products

If you're an affiliate marketer, you know that creating content that drives traffic to your affiliate links is essential to your success. While blog posts and social media updates are effective, videos can be even more powerful.

In this book, we'll discuss how to create videos that promote affiliate products.

Step 1: Research Your Audience

Before you start creating videos, you need to understand your audience. What are their pain points and what do they want to learn? What are their interests and hobbies? What type of content do they consume on YouTube? Understanding your audience is essential to creating videos that will resonate with them.

Step 2: Choose Products to Promote

Once you understand your audience, it's time to choose the products you want to promote. Look for products that align with your niche and offer value to your audience. You want to promote products that you genuinely believe in and that your audience will find helpful.

Step 3: Create High-Quality Videos

When creating videos, quality is key. You don't need to have expensive equipment, but you do need to create videos that are clear and easy to watch. Make sure your lighting and sound are good, and that your videos are well-edited.

Step 4: Make the Product the Focus

When creating videos that promote affiliate products, make sure the product is the focus. You want to show how the product works, its features and benefits, and why your audience should consider purchasing it. However, don't be overly salesy. Your audience wants to learn, not just be sold to.

Step 5: Include Your Affiliate Link

Make sure to include your affiliate link in the video description and in the video itself. This makes it easy for your audience to click through and purchase the product. Be transparent about your affiliate relationship and let your audience know that you'll earn a commission if they make a purchase.

Step 6: Promote Your Videos

Once you've created your videos, it's time to promote them. Share them on social media, embed them in blog posts, and include them in your email newsletter. The more you promote your videos, the more traffic you'll drive to your affiliate links.

In conclusion, creating videos that promote affiliate products is an effective way to drive traffic and earn commissions. By understanding your audience, choosing the right products, and creating high-quality

videos, you can create content that resonates with your viewers and drives them to take action.

4.3 Incorporating affiliate links in your videos

Incorporating affiliate links in your videos is a crucial step in the process of monetizing your YouTube channel. By adding affiliate links to your videos, you can earn a commission on every sale that is made through your link. In this blog post, we will go over some tips and best practices for incorporating affiliate links in your videos.

Be transparent.

It's important to disclose to your viewers that you are using affiliate links in your videos. This will help build trust with your audience and ensure that they know you are being transparent about your motives. You can do this by adding a disclosure statement in the video description or mentioning it in the video itself.

Choose the right products

When selecting products to promote through affiliate links, make sure they align with the interests of your audience. This will increase the likelihood of your viewers clicking on your links and making a purchase. Additionally, it's important to choose products that are relevant to the content of your video.

Use clear calls to action

When incorporating affiliate links in your videos, make sure to use clear calls to action. You can do this by adding a clickable link in the video description, adding a graphic overlay with a call to action, or verbally encouraging your viewers to click on the link.

Place links strategically

The placement of your affiliate links is also important. You want to make sure that the links are easily accessible to your viewers, but not too distracting from the content of your video. A common practice is to place links in the beginning or end of your video, or in a designated section of the video description.

Test and track your results

As with any marketing strategy, it's important to test and track your results. This will allow you to see what works and what doesn't, and make adjustments accordingly. You can track your results using tools such as **Google Analytics or affiliate tracking software**

In conclusion, incorporating affiliate links in your videos is a great way to monetize your YouTube channel.

By following these tips and best practices, you can increase your chances of success and earn a commission on every sale made through your links. Remember to always be transparent with your audience and choose products that align with their interests.

4.4 Strategies for making your content engaging and persuasive

Creating engaging and persuasive content is crucial to the success of your affiliate marketing efforts on YouTube. By providing value to your viewers and presenting affiliate products in an appealing way, you can increase the chances of conversions and earn more commissions. In this article, we'll discuss several strategies that can help you make your content more engaging and persuasive.

Focus on storytelling:

People love stories. By using storytelling in your videos, you can create a connection with your viewers and keep them engaged. Share personal experiences and anecdotes that relate to your niche and the products you're promoting. This can make your videos more relatable and help your viewers see the value in the products you're recommending.

Be honest and transparent:

Being honest and transparent with your audience is crucial for building trust and credibility.

Disclose that you're promoting affiliate products and explain how they can benefit your viewers.

Share your personal experiences with the products and be honest about their pros and cons.

This can help your viewers make an informed decision and increase the likelihood of conversions.

Use visual aids:

Visual aids such as images, graphs, and charts can help illustrate your points and make your content more engaging. Use screenshots or footage of the products you're promoting to show their features and benefits. This can help your viewers get a better understanding of the products and increase their interest in them.

Provide valuable information:

Your viewers come to your channel to learn and get value. By providing valuable information related to your niche, you can establish yourself as an authority and build a loyal audience.

Provide tips, tutorials, and guides related to the products you're promoting. This can help your viewers see the value in the products and increase the likelihood of conversions.

Use a call-to-action:

A call-to-action is a statement that encourages your viewers to take action. Use a call-to-action at the end of your videos to encourage your viewers to click on your affiliate links and make a purchase. Make your call-to-action clear and compelling. Use phrases such as "Click the link below to learn more" or "Get your hands on this product today".

Be creative:

Creativity can help you stand out from the crowd and make your content more engaging. Use humor, animation, or music to add personality and flair to your videos. Experiment with different formats and styles to see what works best for your audience.

Conclusion:

Creating engaging and persuasive content is key to success in affiliate marketing on YouTube.

By using storytelling, being honest and transparent, using visual aids, providing valuable information, using a call-to-action, and being creative, you can increase the chances of conversions and earn more commissions. Remember to focus on providing value to your viewers and building trust and credibility with your audience.

Chapter 5

Growing Your Audience and Building Your Brand

5.1 Promoting your videos on YouTube and other social media channels

Promoting your videos on YouTube and other social media channels is an essential step to ensuring your affiliate marketing efforts reach your target audience. Here are some detailed tips and strategies for promoting your videos effectively:

- **Optimize your video title and description**: Your video title and description should accurately reflect the content of your video and include relevant keywords for search engine optimization (SEO). This will help your video rank higher in search results and attract more views.

- **Use eye-catching thumbnails**: Your video thumbnail is the first thing viewers see when scrolling through YouTube or other social media platforms, so it's important to make it eye-catching and compelling. Use high-quality images and bold, attention-grabbing text to entice viewers to click on your video. Share on social media: Share your videos on social media platforms like Facebook, Twitter, and Instagram to reach a wider audience. You can also use social media ads to target specific demographics and increase visibility.

- **Engage with your audience**: Respond to comments on your videos and social media posts to build relationships with your audience and encourage engagement. This will help foster a community of loyal followers who are more likely to purchase products through your affiliate links.

- **Collaborate with other YouTubers and influencers**: Collaborating with other creators in your niche can help you reach new audiences and increase your exposure. Consider partnering with other YouTubers and influencers on joint projects or promotions to expand your reach and gain more followers.

- **Use email marketing**: Collect email addresses from your viewers and followers to build an email list. You can then use email marketing to promote your videos and affiliate products to your subscribers.

- **Participate in forums and online communities**: Find online forums and communities related to your niche and participate in discussions. This can help establish you as an expert in your field and attract more followers to your YouTube channel.

By implementing these strategies, you can effectively promote your videos and increase your affiliate marketing success on YouTube and other social media channels. Remember to continually monitor your analytics to track your progress and adjust your strategies as needed.

5.2 Building your email list and using it to promote affiliate products

Building your email list and using it to promote affiliate products can be an effective strategy for increasing your affiliate marketing revenue. In this article, we will discuss the benefits of email marketing, how to build your email list, and how to use it to promote affiliate products.

5.3 Benefits of Email Marketing

Email marketing is one of the most effective ways to connect with your audience and build a loyal following. Here are some of the benefits of email marketing for affiliate marketing:

- **Builds Trust**: By regularly sending emails to your subscribers, you can build trust and establish yourself as an authority in your niche.

- **Increases Engagement**: Email marketing allows you to engage with your audience on a more personal level, which can lead to higher engagement rates and increased conversions.
- **Boosts Sales**: By promoting relevant affiliate products to your email list, you can increase your sales and generate a passive income stream.

5.4 How to Build Your Email List

Building an email list requires a consistent effort over time. Here are some effective strategies for growing your email list:

- **Offer an incentive**: Offer a free guide or e-book in exchange for your audience's email address.
- **Use a sign-up form**: Place a sign-up form on your website or YouTube channel to encourage your audience to subscribe to your email list.
- **Host a giveaway**: Host a giveaway or contest and require participants to provide their email address to enter.
- **Promote on social media**: Promote your email list on social media by including a sign-up link in your posts and bio.

- **Collaborate with others**: Collaborate with other YouTubers or influencers in your niche to reach a wider audience and promote your email list.

5.5 How to Use Your Email List to Promote Affiliate Products

Once you have built your email list, you can use it to promote relevant affiliate products. Here are some tips for effectively promoting affiliate products to your email list:

- **Segment your list**: Segment your email list based on your subscribers' interests and preferences to ensure that you are sending them relevant offers.

- **Provide value**: Before promoting an affiliate product, provide value to your subscribers by sharing helpful tips, resources, or information related to your niche.

- **Highlight the benefits**: When promoting affiliate products, highlight the benefits and how they can solve a problem or meet a need for your audience.

- **Use a call-to-action**: Include a clear call-to-action in your email, encouraging your subscribers to click on your affiliate link and make a purchase.

- **Monitor your results**: Monitor your email marketing results to track your open rates, click-through rates, and conversions. Use this data to refine your email marketing strategy and improve your results.

In conclusion, building your email list and using it to promote affiliate products can be an effective strategy for increasing your affiliate marketing revenue. By providing value, segmenting your list, and monitoring your results, you can build a loyal following and generate a passive income stream from your affiliate marketing efforts.

5.6 Strategies for developing a strong brand and establishing credibility

Developing a strong brand and establishing credibility are critical elements of a successful affiliate marketing campaign. Without trust and credibility, it's challenging to attract and retain customers. In this section, we'll discuss the strategies for building a strong brand and establishing credibility.

- **Develop a unique brand identity**: A brand is more than just a logo or a tagline. It's a promise you make to your customers.

Develop a unique brand identity that resonates with your target audience. Your

brand should reflect your values and your mission. This includes creating a consistent visual identity, including your logo, color scheme, and typography.

- **Provide value to your audience**: One of the best ways to establish credibility is by providing value to your audience. Create high-quality content that solves their problems or answers their questions. Offer free resources, such as books, guides, and webinars that are relevant to your audience. This will help you build trust and credibility with your audience.

- **Be authentic and transparent**: Authenticity and transparency are critical in building trust with your audience. Be transparent about your affiliations and disclose any financial relationships with your partners. Provide honest and unbiased reviews of the products and services you promote. This will help you establish credibility and build trust with your audience.

- **Engage with your audience**: Engaging with your audience is an excellent way to build relationships and establish credibility. Respond to comments and questions on your videos and social media posts. This shows that you value your audience's opinions and are willing to engage with them.

- **Use social proof**: Social proof is a powerful tool for establishing credibility. This includes customer reviews, case studies, and testimonials. Incorporate social proof into your content and promotions. This will help you establish credibility and build trust with your audience.

- **Partner with other credible brands**: Partnering with other credible brands can also help you establish credibility. Identify brands that share your values and mission and are relevant to your audience. Collaborate on content and promotions to reach a broader audience and establish credibility with their followers.

In summary, building a strong brand and establishing credibility are critical to the success of your affiliate marketing campaign. By developing a unique brand identity, providing value to your audience, being authentic and transparent, engaging with your audience, using social proof, and partnering with other credible brands, you can establish credibility and build trust with your audience.

Chapter 6

Analyzing and Optimizing Your Results

6.1 Tracking your affiliate marketing performance

Tracking your affiliate marketing performance is an essential step in optimizing your strategy and maximizing your earnings. By monitoring your results, you can identify what works and what doesn't, and make data-driven decisions to improve your performance.

Here are some key metrics and tools you can use to track your affiliate marketing performance:

- **Click-through rate (CTR)**: This metric measures the percentage of clicks on your affiliate links compared to the number of impressions. You can track your CTR using Google Analytics or the tracking tools provided by your affiliate network.

- **Conversion rate**: This metric measures the percentage of visitors who click on your affiliate link and make a purchase. You can track your conversion rate using tracking pixels or conversion tracking tools provided by your affiliate network.

- **Earnings per click (EPC)**: This metric measures the average earnings you receive per click on your affiliate link. You can calculate your EPC by dividing your total earnings by the number of clicks.

- **Revenue**: This metric measures the total amount of money you earn from your affiliate marketing activities. You can track your revenue using your affiliate network's reporting tools.

- **ROI**: This metric measures the return on investment of your affiliate marketing activities. You can calculate your ROI by subtracting your costs from your revenue and dividing the result by your costs.

To track your performance effectively, you can use tools such as Google Analytics, affiliate network reporting tools, and third-party tracking software. These tools allow you to monitor your metrics in real-time, analyze your results, and identify areas for improvement.

In addition to tracking your performance, it's also important to regularly review your affiliate programs and networks to ensure they continue to align with your niche and audience. You may also want to consider experimenting with different types of affiliate products and promotional strategies to see what works best for your audience.

By tracking your performance and continually refining your strategy, you can optimize your affiliate marketing efforts and maximize your earnings over time.

6.2 Optimizing your content and promotion strategies

Once you have established your YouTube channel, developed your niche, and identified your affiliate products, it's time to optimize your content and promotion strategies to drive traffic and maximize conversions. In this guide, we will explore some key strategies to help you achieve these goals.

Use keyword research to optimize your video titles and descriptions

Keyword research is an essential tool for improving the visibility of your videos in search results.

By identifying the keywords and phrases that your target audience is searching for, you can optimize your video titles, descriptions, and tags to make it easier for them to find your content.

To conduct keyword research, start by brainstorming some broad topics related to your niche.

Then, use a keyword research tool like Google Keyword Planner or SEMrush to identify the specific keywords and phrases that people are searching for in relation to those topics.

Incorporate these keywords into your video titles, descriptions, and tags to improve your search rankings and attract more viewers.

Optimize your video thumbnails for maximum click-through rates

Your video thumbnails are the first thing that viewers see when browsing through YouTube search results or suggested videos. As such, they play

a critical role in determining whether or not someone clicks through to watch your content.

To optimize your video thumbnails, use high-quality images that are relevant to the content of your video. Incorporate text and other visual elements to make the thumbnail eye-catching and informative. Test different thumbnail designs to see which ones generate the highest click-through rates.

Use calls-to-action to encourage viewers to take action calls-to-action (CTAs) are a crucial element of any successful affiliate marketing campaign. Use CTAs throughout your videos to encourage viewers to take specific actions, such as clicking on a link, subscribing to your channel, or leaving a comment.

Be specific and direct in your CTAs, and make sure they align with the goals of your affiliate marketing campaign. For example, if your goal is to drive traffic to a specific product page, use a CTA that encourages viewers to click on the link in your video description to learn more about that product.

Leverage social media to promote your videos and affiliate products

Social media is a powerful tool for promoting your YouTube channel and driving traffic to your affiliate products. Share your videos on your social media profiles, and encourage your followers to like, comment, and share them.

You can also use social media to build relationships with your audience and promote your affiliate products in a more indirect way. For example, share helpful tips and insights related to your niche, and incorporate links to your affiliate products where appropriate.

Continuously test and optimize your strategies for maximum results

Finally, it's important to remember that affiliate marketing is an ongoing process of testing and optimization. Continuously monitor your performance metrics, such as click-through rates and conversion rates, and experiment with different content and promotion strategies to see what works best.

By implementing these strategies and continually optimizing your approach, you can maximize the impact of your affiliate marketing efforts and drive significant revenue through your YouTube channel.

6.3 Scaling your affiliate marketing efforts for maximum results

Affiliate marketing is an excellent way to earn passive income, and if you've been successful at it, you might be wondering how to take your efforts to the next level. Scaling your affiliate marketing efforts can lead to even greater returns, but it requires a strategic approach. In this book, we'll explore some of the best strategies for scaling your affiliate marketing efforts for maximum results.

- **Expand your content offerings**: One of the most effective ways to scale your affiliate marketing efforts is to create more content. This includes blog posts, videos, social media content, email newsletters, and more. By expanding your content offerings, you'll increase your reach and attract a larger audience. Make sure to focus on quality over quantity, and optimize your content for your target audience.

- **Utilize paid advertising**: While organic reach is great, paid advertising can take your affiliate marketing efforts to the next level. This includes using platforms like Facebook Ads and Google Ads to promote your content and affiliate products. Make sure to carefully target your ads to ensure you're reaching the right audience, and monitor your campaigns closely to ensure you're getting a good return on your investment.

- **Partner with other affiliates**: Collaboration is key when it comes to scaling your affiliate marketing efforts. Consider partnering with other affiliates who have a similar target audience and creating joint content or promotions. This can help you reach a wider audience and earn more commissions.

- **Leverage automation**: As your affiliate marketing efforts grow, it can be challenging to manage everything manually. Consider leveraging automation tools like email autoresponders and social media schedulers to streamline your workflow and save time.

- **Diversify your affiliate product offerings**: While it's important to focus on products that align with your niche and audience, diversifying your affiliate product offerings can help you maximize your earnings. Look for complementary products or services that your audience may be interested in and consider promoting those as well.

- **Analyze your data**: To effectively scale your affiliate marketing efforts, you need to understand what's working and what's not. Take the time to analyze your data and metrics, including click-through rates, conversion rates, and revenue earned. Use this information to optimize your content and promotional strategies.

- **Continuously learn and improve**: Finally, it's important to continuously learn and improve your affiliate marketing strategies. Keep up with industry trends, attend webinars and conferences, and network with other affiliates to stay on top of your game.

In conclusion, scaling your affiliate marketing efforts takes time and effort, but the rewards can be significant. By expanding your content offerings, utilizing paid advertising, partnering with other affiliates, leveraging automation, diversifying your affiliate product offerings, analyzing your data, and continuously learning and improving, you can take your affiliate marketing earnings to the next level.

Chapter 7

Advanced Affiliate Marketing Techniques

7.1 Developing strategic partnerships with other YouTubers and influencers

Developing strategic partnerships with other YouTubers and influencers can be a highly effective way to increase your visibility, credibility, and reach as an affiliate marketer on YouTube. By collaborating with other creators who share your niche and target audience, you can tap into their existing audience and leverage their influence to boost your own authority and credibility.

Here are some key steps to developing successful partnerships with other YouTubers and influencers:

- **Identify potential partners**: Start by researching other YouTubers and influencers in your niche who have a significant following and engagement. Look for creators who share your values and target audience, and who have a strong online presence and reputation.

- **Build relationships**: Reach out to potential partners and start building a relationship by engaging with their content, leaving thoughtful comments, and sharing their videos with your own audience. Consider offering to collaborate on a project or co-host a live event together.

- **Provide value**: When working with other creators, it's important to focus on providing value to their audience, rather than just promoting your own products or services. Think about how you can contribute to their content and add value to their viewers, whether it's by sharing your expertise, providing insider tips, or offering exclusive discounts or promotions.

- **Negotiate terms**: Once you've established a relationship with a potential partner, it's important to negotiate the terms of your partnership upfront. Be clear about your goals and expectations, and discuss how you will promote each other's content and products.

- **Track results**: As with any marketing strategy, it's important to track the results of your partnerships to ensure they are delivering the expected ROI. Use tracking tools to monitor traffic, clicks, and conversions from your partner's content, and adjust your strategy as needed to optimize your results.

Overall, developing strategic partnerships with other YouTubers and influencers can be a highly effective way to grow your audience, boost your credibility, and increase your revenue as an affiliate marketer on YouTube. By focusing on building genuine relationships and providing value to your partners and their audience, you can create a win-win situation that benefits everyone involved.

7.2 Creating your own affiliate products and programs

Creating Your Own Affiliate Products and Programs: A Detailed Review

Affiliate marketing has become a popular way to make money online, and for good reason. With the right strategy, it can be a highly lucrative source of income. One way to take your affiliate marketing efforts to the next level is to create your own affiliate products and programs.

When you create your own products, you have more control over the marketing and pricing, and you can also offer affiliate commissions to others who promote your products. This can be a win-win situation for both you and your affiliates.

Here are some key steps to consider when creating your own affiliate products and programs:

Identify a Need in Your Niche

The first step in creating your own affiliate products and programs is to identify a need in your niche. What products or services are your audience looking for that they can't find elsewhere?

What problem can you solve for them? Once you have identified a need, you can start brainstorming ideas for products that would meet that need.

Choose a Product Type

Once you have identified a need and generated product ideas, you need to choose a product type. There are several types of products you can create, including digital products like e-books, courses, or software, and physical products like merchandise or subscription boxes. Choose a product type that aligns with your niche and audience, and that you have the expertise and resources to create.

Develop Your Product

Now that you have chosen a product type, it's time to develop your product. This involves creating the content, designing the product, and developing any necessary software or tools.

Depending on your product type and your own skills and resources, you may need to outsource some of the work to freelancers or agencies.

Set Your Price and Commission Rate

Once your product is ready, you need to set a price that reflects its value and covers your costs.

You also need to decide on the commission rate you will offer to affiliates who promote your product. This should be competitive with other affiliate programs in your niche, and should provide enough incentive for affiliates to promote your product.

Create Your Affiliate Program

Now it's time to create your affiliate program. You can use affiliate software or services to set up your program, or you can create your own system using tracking links and payment processing.

Your affiliate program should include clear terms and conditions, and should provide affiliates with the resources they need to promote your product effectively.

Recruit Affiliates

Once your affiliate program is set up, you need to recruit affiliates to promote your product. You can reach out to other YouTubers and influencers in your niche, or you can advertise your affiliate program on your website or social media channels. You should also provide affiliates with promotional materials like banners, social media graphics, and email templates to make it easy for them to promote your product.

Monitor and Optimize Your Program

Finally, it's important to monitor and optimize your affiliate program to ensure it's performing as well as possible. Keep track of your sales and commission payouts, and look for ways to improve your program. This might include adjusting your commission rate, creating new promotional materials, or offering bonuses to top-performing affiliates.

Creating your own affiliate products and programs can be a highly effective way to boost your affiliate marketing income and establish yourself as a thought leader in your niche. By following these key steps, you can create a profitable product and attract top-performing affiliates to promote it.

7.3 How to use data and analytics to drive your affiliate marketing strategies

Using data and analytics is a crucial part of any successful affiliate marketing strategy. By tracking and analyzing your performance metrics, you can make informed decisions about where to focus your efforts and optimize your campaigns for maximum results. Here are some key ways to use data and analytics to drive your affiliate marketing strategies:

Track your affiliate links: One of the most basic forms of data tracking in affiliate marketing is monitoring the performance of your affiliate links. By using tools like Google Analytics or affiliate network dashboards, you can track how many clicks and conversions your links are generating.

This can help you identify which products and promotions are resonating with your audience and adjust your strategies accordingly.

Analyze audience demographics: Understanding who your audience is and what they are interested in can help you tailor your content and promotions to their specific needs and preferences. By using data analytics tools like Google Analytics, you can track metrics like age,

gender, location, and interests to gain insights into your audience's behavior and preferences.

Test and optimize your content: A/B testing is a powerful tool for optimizing your content and promotions for maximum performance. By creating different versions of your content and tracking their performance metrics, you can identify which variations are generating the most clicks, conversions, and revenue. This can help you refine your content and promotions over time to maximize your ROI.

Monitor competition and trends: Keeping an eye on your competitors and industry trends can help you identify new opportunities and stay ahead of the curve. By using tools like SEMrush or BuzzSumo, you can track your competitors' content and promotions, as well as monitor industry keywords and trends to identify new niches and audiences to target.

Use retargeting and remarketing: Retargeting and remarketing are powerful techniques for re-engaging with users who have shown an interest in your products or promotions. By using data analytics tools to track user behavior on your website or social media channels, you can create targeted ad campaigns that reach users who have already interacted with your brand.

This can help you increase your conversion rates and generate more revenue from your affiliate marketing efforts.

Overall, using data and analytics is essential for driving your affiliate marketing strategies and maximizing your results. By tracking and analyzing your performance metrics, you can make informed decisions about where to focus your efforts and optimize your campaigns for maximum ROI.

Chapter 8

Conclusion

8.1 Resources and tools for further learning and growth on affiliate marketing on YouTube

If you're interested in learning more about affiliate marketing on YouTube, there are many resources and tools available to help you get started and grow your business. Here are a few recommendations:

YouTube Creator Academy: This is a free resource provided by YouTube that offers a wide range of courses and tutorials on creating and optimizing content, growing your audience, and monetizing your channel through affiliate marketing and other means.

Affiliate marketing networks: There are many affiliate marketing networks available, including Amazon Associates, ShareASale, Commission Junction, and ClickBank, among others. These networks offer access to a wide range of affiliate products and services that you can promote on your channel.

Affiliate marketing plugins and tools: There are many plugins and tools available that can help you optimize your affiliate marketing efforts on YouTube. These include tools for tracking clicks and conversions, managing affiliate links, and more.

YouTube SEO tools: To maximize your reach and visibility on YouTube, you'll want to use tools to optimize your videos and channel for search engines. Some popular tools for this include TubeBuddy, VidIQ, and Morningfame.

Online courses and coaching: If you're serious about building a successful affiliate marketing business on YouTube, you may want to consider investing in online courses or coaching programs that offer more personalized guidance and support.

Remember, the key to success with affiliate marketing on YouTube is to create high-quality, engaging content that resonates with your audience and promotes products and services that they are genuinely interested in. By using the right resources and tools, and continually testing and refining your strategies, you can build a profitable affiliate marketing business on YouTube over time.

Affiliate Marketing Automation:

Using Tools and Software To Automate Various Aspects of the Affiliate Marketing Process, Such As Tracking, Reporting, and Payment Processing

Chapter 1

Introduction

1.1 Explanation of affiliate marketing automation

Affiliate marketing automation involves using various tools and software to streamline and automate the different aspects of affiliate marketing. It uses technology to improve efficiency, reduce manual labor, and make the entire process faster and more effective.

One of the key features of affiliate marketing automation is the ability to track and analyze data.

This data can include information about sales, clicks, commissions, and more. By using this data, affiliate marketers can gain insights into the behavior of their customers and make data-driven decisions about which products to promote and how to optimize their marketing efforts.

Another important aspect of affiliate marketing automation is the ability to automate tasks such as email marketing, social media promotion, and lead generation. This can help save time and resources, while still maintaining a high level of engagement with potential customers.

Other features of affiliate marketing automation may include integration with various platforms, such as e-commerce platforms, social media networks, and advertising networks. This allows for seamless integration and management of different aspects of the affiliate marketing process.

Ultimately, affiliate marketing automation can help affiliate marketers achieve greater efficiency, scalability, and profitability. By leveraging technology to streamline and automate tasks, affiliate marketers can focus on creating high-quality content and building strong relationships with their audience, while still driving revenue and maximizing profits.

1.2 Why automation is important for affiliate marketers

Automation is important for affiliate marketers because it allows them to streamline their processes and save time while also increasing efficiency and productivity. With automation tools, affiliate marketers can automate various tasks such as email marketing, social media posting, lead nurturing, and more. This helps to reduce manual workloads and increase the speed and accuracy of various processes, freeing up time to focus on other important aspects of the business, such as developing strategies and building relationships with partners.

Automation also helps to improve the accuracy and consistency of campaigns, leading to better results and higher ROI.

1.3 Overview of what the book will cover

Affiliate marketing has become an increasingly popular way for individuals and businesses to earn income online. By promoting products and services through affiliate links, marketers can earn a commission on each sale made through their referral. However, managing multiple affiliate programs, tracking commissions, and optimizing marketing campaigns can quickly become overwhelming, especially as a marketer's reach grows. That's where affiliate marketing automation comes in.

Affiliate marketing automation refers to the use of technology and tools to streamline and optimize the affiliate marketing process. It involves automating tasks such as lead generation, email marketing, and tracking, allowing marketers to focus on creating quality content and building relationships with their audience.

In this book, we will explore the different aspects of affiliate marketing automation, including the benefits, tools and technologies available, and best practices for implementation. Whether you are just starting out as an affiliate marketer or looking to scale your efforts, this guide will provide valuable insights and strategies for optimizing your affiliate marketing workflow.

Affiliate marketing can be an incredibly profitable way to make money online, but it can also be time-consuming and difficult to manage. This is where automation comes in. By automating certain tasks and processes, affiliate marketers can save time and increase efficiency, ultimately leading to greater profits.

There are many different tools and techniques that can be used to automate various aspects of affiliate marketing, from email campaigns to social media posts. By using automation, marketers can reach a wider audience, increase their conversion rates, and ultimately make more money with less effort.

However, it's important to note that automation should not be used as a replacement for human interaction and engagement. While automation can handle many of the routine tasks associated with affiliate marketing, it's still important to build relationships with your audience and provide valuable content and insights that can't be automated.

In this book, we'll explore the various ways that affiliate marketers can use automation to streamline their efforts and maximize their profits. We'll cover everything from email marketing and social media automation to affiliate tracking and reporting. By the end of this book, you'll have a solid understanding of how to implement automation in your affiliate marketing strategy, and the tools and resources you need to get started.

Chapter 2

Understanding Affiliate Marketing Automation

2.1 Automation and how it applies to affiliate marketing

Automation is the use of technology to automate and streamline repetitive tasks or processes.

In the context of affiliate marketing, automation refers to the use of software, tools, and systems to automate various tasks, such as lead capture, email marketing, content creation, social media marketing, and analytics.

Affiliate marketing automation is particularly useful for managing large affiliate marketing campaigns and increasing efficiency. By automating certain tasks, affiliate marketers can save time, reduce errors, and improve overall campaign performance.

For example, an affiliate marketer can use automation software to track the performance of various affiliate links, automatically generate affiliate reports, and send targeted email campaigns to specific audiences based on their behaviors and interests.

Overall, affiliate marketing automation helps marketers streamline their workflows, optimize their campaigns, and increase their revenue. It also allows them to focus on high-level tasks, such as developing new strategies and partnerships, rather than being bogged down by tedious administrative tasks.

2.2 Examples of automation tools and technologies used in affiliate marketing

There are a variety of automation tools and technologies used in affiliate marketing to streamline and optimize various tasks and processes. Here are some examples:

- **Affiliate Tracking Software**: This tool helps to track clicks, leads, and sales generated by affiliates. It helps merchants to track the performance of their affiliates and also helps affiliates to track their commissions and earnings.

- **Email Marketing Automation**: This tool automates the process of sending emails to subscribers, promoting products, and nurturing leads. It helps to build relationships with subscribers and increase the chances of making sales.

- **Chatbot**: A chatbot is a software application that automates communication with customers. It can be used to provide customer support, answer frequently asked questions, and promote products to customers.

- **Social Media Automation**: This tool helps to automate social media posts, schedule content, and monitor social media activity. It helps to save time and increase the efficiency of social media marketing.

- **Landing Page Optimization**: This tool automates the process of creating and testing landing pages. It helps to improve the conversion rate of landing pages and increase the chances of making sales.

- **Data Analytics**: This tool automates the process of data collection, analysis, and reporting. It helps to track the performance of campaigns, optimize strategies, and make data-driven decisions.

Overall, these tools and technologies help to save time, increase efficiency, and improve the performance of affiliate marketing campaigns. They are essential for scaling up affiliate marketing efforts and achieving maximum results.

2.3 Advantages and disadvantages of automation in affiliate marketing

Advantages of automation in affiliate marketing:

- **Saves time and increases efficiency**: One of the biggest benefits of automation in affiliate marketing is that it can save a lot of time for affiliate marketers. Tasks such as data entry, lead nurturing, and

reporting can be automated, freeing up time for marketers to focus on more important tasks.

- **Improves accuracy**: Automation tools can help eliminate human errors in data entry and other repetitive tasks, ensuring that data is more accurate and reliable.

- **Increases scalability**: Automation allows affiliate marketers to scale their efforts without increasing their workload. As the volume of leads, sales, and commissions increases, automation tools can handle the increased workload.

- **Provides real-time insights**: Automation tools can provide real-time insights into key metrics such as clicks, conversions, and revenue. This can help affiliate marketers make data-driven decisions and optimize their campaigns for better results.

Disadvantages of automation in affiliate marketing:

- **Can be expensive**: Many automation tools and technologies can be expensive, especially for small affiliate marketers. The cost of implementing automation can sometimes outweigh the benefits.

- **Lack of personal touch**: Automated emails and messages may lack the personal touch that comes with human interaction, which can be a disadvantage for some customers.

- **Dependence on technology**: Affiliate marketers who rely heavily on automation tools may become too dependent on technology and lose the ability to make decisions based on human intuition and experience.

- **Limited customization**: Some automation tools may not offer the level of customization that some affiliate marketers need to achieve their specific goals. This can limit the effectiveness of automation in some cases.

Chapter 3

Setting Up Your Automated Affiliate Marketing System

3.1 Identifying goals and objectives for your automated system

Identifying goals and objectives for your automated system is a crucial step in affiliate marketing automation. Without clear goals, it can be challenging to determine what you want to automate and how to measure the success of your efforts.

When setting goals for your automated system, it's important to think about what you want to achieve. For example, your goals could include:

Increasing conversions: If your main goal is to increase conversions, you may want to focus on automating processes that help to move customers through the sales funnel more quickly.

- **Improving customer retention**: If you want to improve customer retention, you may want to focus on automating processes that help to nurture your relationships with customers over time.

- **Enhancing the customer experience**: If you want to enhance the customer experience, you may want to focus on automating processes that provide personalized recommendations or targeted content to your audience.

Once you have identified your goals, you can begin to determine the metrics that you will use to measure success. For example, if your goal is to increase conversions, you might measure success by looking at the conversion rate for your automated system. If your goal is to improve customer retention, you might measure success by looking at the customer retention rate.

By identifying your goals and objectives for your automated system, you can ensure that your efforts are focused on achieving the outcomes that matter most to your business.

3.2 Determining which tasks can be automated

When implementing an affiliate marketing automation system, it is important to determine which tasks can be automated to streamline the process and save time. Here are some examples of tasks that can be automated:

- **Email marketing**: Email marketing is an effective way to promote affiliate products to your audience. By automating your email marketing campaigns, you can send out targeted messages at specific intervals, such as welcome emails, promotional emails, and abandoned cart reminders.

- **Social media posting**: Social media is a great way to reach a wider audience and promote your affiliate products. Automation tools can help you schedule posts in advance, ensuring that your content is published at the right time to reach your target audience.

- **Affiliate link insertion**: Instead of manually inserting affiliate links into your content, automation tools can help you insert them automatically. This saves you time and ensures that all of your content includes affiliate links, maximizing your earning potential.

- **Data analysis**: Automation tools can also help you analyze data, such as click-through rates, conversion rates, and revenue generated from each affiliate product. This allows you to identify which products are most profitable and adjust your marketing strategies accordingly.

- **Affiliate program management**: If you manage multiple affiliate programs, automation tools can help you keep track of your earnings, commission rates, and other important metrics. This can help you optimize your performance and maximize your earning potential.

Overall, automation can help you save time and increase your revenue by streamlining your affiliate marketing tasks and allowing you to focus on high-value activities such as creating content and building relationships with your audience.

3.3 Choosing the right automation tools for your system

Choosing the right automation tools for your affiliate marketing system is crucial to its success.

Here are some factors to consider when selecting automation tools:

- **Functionality**: Choose tools that can automate the tasks you need to perform. For example, if you need to schedule social media posts, look for a tool that can do this.

- **Integration**: Consider how well the tools you choose integrate with each other and with the platforms you use. For example, if you use WordPress for your website and Mailchimp for email marketing, make sure the automation tools you choose can integrate with these platforms.

- **Ease of use**: Look for tools that are user-friendly and intuitive. You don't want to waste time learning how to use complicated software.

- **Cost**: Consider the cost of the tools you choose. While some tools may be expensive, they may offer features that can save you time and money in the long run.

- **Customer support**: Look for tools that offer excellent customer support, such as live chat or phone support. You may run into problems when using automation tools, so having good customer support is important.

By considering these factors, you can choose the right automation tools for your affiliate marketing system and streamline your workflow for maximum efficiency.

3.4 Creating a workflow for your automated system

Creating a workflow for your affiliate marketing automation system is an important step towards achieving your marketing goals and objectives. A workflow is essentially a series of steps or processes that your system will follow to automate certain tasks, such as lead generation, lead nurturing, and product promotions. Here are some key considerations when creating a workflow for your affiliate marketing automation system:

- **Identify your objectives**: Before you start designing your workflow, you need to identify your marketing goals and objectives. For instance, if you want to increase sales for a particular product, you might want to design a workflow that focuses on generating more leads and nurturing them with targeted content and promotions.

- **Map out your customer journey**: Once you have identified your objectives, you need to map out your customer journey. This involves understanding your target audience and the stages they go through before making a purchase. By understanding the customer

  journey, you can design a workflow that targets each stage of the journey with relevant content and promotions.

- **Design your workflow**: Once you have mapped out your customer journey, you can start designing your workflow. This involves creating a series of steps or processes that your system will follow to automate tasks such as lead generation, lead nurturing, and product promotions.

You can use automation tools and technologies such as email marketing software, landing page builders, and social media management platforms to streamline your workflow and make it more efficient.

- **Test and refine**: Once you have designed your workflow, you need to test it to ensure that it is effective in achieving your marketing goals and objectives. You can use analytics and tracking tools to monitor the performance of your workflow and make adjustments as needed.

Overall, creating a workflow for your affiliate marketing automation system is essential for achieving your marketing goals and objectives. By mapping out your customer journey, designing your workflow, and testing and refining it, you can create an effective automated system that generates more leads and sales for your affiliate products.

3.5 Choosing the right automation tools for your system

Choosing the right automation tools for your affiliate marketing system is crucial to its success.

Here are some factors to consider when selecting automation tools:

- **Functionality**: Choose tools that can automate the tasks you need to perform. For example, if you need to schedule social media posts, look for a tool that can do this.

- **Integration**: Consider how well the tools you choose integrate with each other and with the platforms you use. For example, if you use WordPress for your website and Mailchimp for email marketing, make sure the automation tools you choose can integrate with these platforms.

- **Ease of use**: Look for tools that are user-friendly and intuitive. You don't want to waste time learning how to use complicated software.

- **Cost**: Consider the cost of the tools you choose. While some tools may be expensive, they may offer features that can save you time and money in the long run.

- **Customer support**: Look for tools that offer excellent customer support, such as live chat or phone support. You may run into problems when using automation tools, so having good customer support is important.

By considering these factors, you can choose the right automation tools for your affiliate marketing system and streamline your workflow for maximum efficiency.

Chapter 4

Optimizing Your Automated Affiliate Marketing System

4.1 Analyzing and measuring the performance of your automated campaigns

Analyzing and measuring the performance of your automated campaigns is crucial to understand how effective your automation strategy is and to make data-driven decisions to optimize it. Here are some important steps to take:

- **Define Key Performance Indicators (KPIs)**: Before you begin measuring performance, it's important to define what success looks like for your automated campaigns. This could include metrics such as conversion rate, click-through rate, revenue generated, and more.

- **Use Analytics Tools**: Utilize analytics tools such as Google Analytics, Hotjar, or Mixpanel to track and analyze your data. These tools can provide valuable insights into user behavior, conversion paths, and more.

- **A/B Testing**: Testing different variations of your automated campaigns can help you determine what works and what doesn't. A/B testing can be used to test different email subject lines, landing pages, or even social media ads.

- **Monitor Metrics Regularly**: Make it a habit to regularly check in on your KPIs and other important metrics to identify any trends or changes. This can help you make informed decisions about how to adjust your automation strategy.

- **Continuously Optimize**: Use the insights you gather from analyzing your data to continuously optimize your automated campaigns. This could involve adjusting your targeting, changing your messaging, or experimenting with different automation tools.

By following these steps, you can gain a deeper understanding of how your automated campaigns are performing and take action to improve their effectiveness over time.

4.2 Testing and refining your automated campaigns for better results

Testing and refining your automated campaigns is a crucial step in maximizing the effectiveness of your affiliate marketing automation system. Here are some tips on how to do it:

- **Define your testing goals**: Determine what you want to achieve with your testing, whether it's improving conversion rates, increasing click-through rates, or something else.

- **Start with small changes**: Test one element of your campaign at a time to isolate the impact of each change.

- **Use A/B testing**: Compare two versions of your campaign to see which one performs better. You can test different variations of your email subject lines, call-to-action buttons, landing pages, and more.

- **Monitor your metrics**: Keep track of your key performance indicators (KPIs) like open rates, click-through rates, conversion rates, and revenue. Analyze the data to identify patterns and trends.

- **Refine your campaigns**: Use the insights gained from your testing to make changes and improvements to your automated campaigns. This could involve tweaking your email copy, redesigning your landing pages, or adjusting your targeting.

- **Continuously iterate**: Automation is an ongoing process, so it's important to continuously monitor and refine your campaigns to ensure optimal performance.

By testing and refining your automated campaigns, you can optimize your system for maximum results and increase your affiliate marketing success.

4.3 Identifying areas for improvement and adjusting your system accordingly

When it comes to affiliate marketing automation, identifying areas for improvement and adjusting your system accordingly is a critical step to achieving long-term success. By analyzing your campaign's performance and identifying areas where your automated system could be optimized, you can ensure that your system is continually evolving and improving.

One approach to identifying areas for improvement is to review your campaign's performance data on a regular basis. Look at metrics such as click-through rates, conversion rates, and revenue generated to identify areas that are underperforming. You can then use this information to adjust your automated system to address these issues.

Another approach is to solicit feedback from your audience and customers. This could involve conducting surveys or focus groups to gather information about their experience with your automated system. Use this feedback to identify pain points and opportunities for improvement.

It's also important to keep up-to-date with the latest automation tools and technologies. As new tools become available, evaluate whether they could improve your existing system or provide additional benefits. However, be cautious not to introduce too many changes at once, as this could negatively impact your campaign's performance.

Finally, don't be afraid to experiment and try new things. Testing different approaches and refining your system based on the results is key to achieving the best possible performance.

Keep in mind that automation is not a one-and-done solution, and requires ongoing effort to ensure that it continues to deliver results.

Chapter 6

Scaling Your Automated Affiliate Marketing Efforts

6.1 Strategies for expanding your automated campaigns to reach more people

Expanding your automated campaigns is essential to reaching more people and increasing conversions. Here are some strategies to consider: Expand your target audience: Use your automated system to identify new target audiences that fit your ideal customer profile. You can use data analytics tools to analyze the behaviors and interests of your current customers and find similar audiences to target with your campaigns.

- **Diversify your marketing channels**: Your automated system can also be used to promote your affiliate products on other marketing channels beyond YouTube. Consider expanding to other social media platforms like Facbook, Twitter, and Instagram, as well as email marketing and paid advertising.

- **Offer incentives**: Incentives such as discounts, free trials, or bonus products can motivate potential customers to take action and make a purchase. Use your automated system to identify where these incentives will be most effective, and adjust your campaigns accordingly.

- **Use retargeting**: Retargeting is a powerful strategy that uses cookies to track users who have visited your website or viewed your videos, and then targets them with relevant ads. Use your automated system to set up retargeting campaigns to recapture lost leads and increase conversions.

- **Collaborate with other brands**: Partnering with other brands that complement your niche can help you reach a wider audience and increase sales. Use your automated system to identify potential partners and streamline the collaboration process.

By implementing these strategies, you can maximize the effectiveness of your automated campaigns and achieve greater success in your affiliate marketing efforts.

6.2 Creating partnerships and collaborations to increase your reach

Creating partnerships and collaborations can be an effective way to increase your reach and drive more traffic to your website or offers through affiliate marketing.

Here are some strategies for building partnerships and collaborations:

- **Reach out to other affiliate marketers**: Look for other affiliate marketers who are targeting the same audience as you, but who may not be promoting the same products as you. Reach out to them and explore the possibility of cross-promotion, where you promote their products and they promote yours.

- **Collaborate with influencers**: Influencers are social media personalities who have a large following and can influence the buying decisions of their followers. Identify influencers who align with your niche and audience and collaborate with them to promote your products.

- **Partner with brands**: Partnering with brands can be an effective way to increase your reach and build your credibility as an affiliate marketer. Look for brands that align with your niche and audience, and reach out to them to explore partnership opportunities.

- **Offer incentives**: To incentivize other affiliate marketers or influencers to collaborate with you, consider offering them a commission or bonus for every sale that they generate through their promotion of your products.

- **Create content together**: Collaborate with other affiliate marketers, influencers, or brands to create content that promotes your products.

This could include videos, blog posts, social media posts, or even a podcast.

By building partnerships and collaborations, you can tap into new audiences and increase your reach, while also building your credibility and authority as an affiliate marketer.

6.3 Tools and resources for scaling your automated affiliate marketing efforts

There are several tools and resources that can help you scale your automated affiliate marketing efforts. Here are some of them:

- **Affiliate networks**: Joining affiliate networks can give you access to a wide range of affiliate programs and products to promote. Some popular affiliate networks include Commission Junction, ShareASale, and Rakuten Marketing.

- **Email marketing platforms**: Email marketing is an important component of any automated affiliate marketing system. There are several email marketing platforms that can help you automate your email campaigns, such as Mailchimp, AWeber, and Constant Contact.

- **Social media management tools**: Social media is another important channel for promoting your affiliate products. Social media management tools like Hootsuite, Buffer, and Sprout Social can help you manage your social media accounts, schedule posts, and track your social media performance.

- **Landing page builders**: Creating effective landing pages is essential for converting your traffic into sales. Landing page builders like Leadpages, Unbounce, and Instapage can help you create high-converting landing pages without any coding skills.

- **Analytics tools**: Analytics tools like Google Analytics, Mixpanel, and Kissmetrics can help you track and measure the performance of your automated campaigns. These tools can help you identify areas for improvement and optimize your campaigns for better results.

- **Marketing automation software**: Marketing automation software like HubSpot, Marketo, and Pardot can help you automate your entire marketing process, from lead generation to lead nurturing to sales. These tools can help you save time, improve efficiency, and increase your ROI.

- **Affiliate marketing courses and training programs**: There are several affiliate marketing courses and training programs available online that can help you improve your affiliate marketing skills and learn new strategies for scaling your campaigns. Some popular courses include Affiliate Marketing Mastery, Authority Hacker Pro, and Commission Hero.

By using these tools and resources, you can automate and scale your affiliate marketing efforts and achieve better results in less time.

Chapter 7

Challenges and Solutions for Affiliate Marketing Automation

7.1 Common challenges faced in affiliate marketing automation

Affiliate marketing automation can be a powerful tool for boosting productivity and profitability, but it also presents some challenges. Here are some of the most common challenges that affiliate marketers face when implementing automation:

- **Technical expertise**: Affiliate marketing automation often requires a high level of technical expertise, such as programming skills or knowledge of API integrations.

- **Data management**: With large amounts of data being processed and analyzed, it's important to have a solid system in place for managing and storing that data.

- **Integration issues**: Different software and systems may not always be compatible with each other, which can make integration and automation difficult.

- **Lack of customization**: Some automation tools may not allow for enough customization, which can limit their usefulness for specific affiliate marketing needs.

- **Cost:** Implementing automation tools can come with a high cost, both in terms of purchasing the tools themselves and in paying for technical support and maintenance.

- **Legal and ethical concerns**: Automated systems must comply with various laws and ethical standards, such as data privacy regulations and rules against spamming.

To overcome these challenges, it's important to carefully evaluate your needs and goals before selecting automation tools. It's also crucial to invest in training and support to ensure that you can effectively implement and manage your automated system. Finally, regularly reviewing and adjusting your strategies can help ensure that your automated campaigns continue to deliver results over time.

7.2 Solutions for overcoming these challenges and ensuring success

There are several challenges that affiliate marketers may face when implementing automation in their campaigns. These challenges include: Technical difficulties: Automation tools and systems can be complex, and it can be challenging to set them up correctly. Technical glitches or errors may also occur, leading to a breakdown in the automation process.

- **Lack of personalization**: Automated systems can feel impersonal, which can lead to lower engagement and conversion rates.

- **Data accuracy and quality**: Automated systems rely on data to function, and if the data is incorrect or outdated, it can lead to inaccurate targeting or ineffective campaigns.
- **Over-automation**: Over-automation can lead to a lack of control over the campaigns, resulting in less-effective targeting and less relevant messaging.

To overcome these challenges, affiliate marketers can take several steps, including:

- **Partnering with experts**: Working with experts who have experience in implementing automation systems can help to overcome technical challenges and ensure the automation process runs smoothly.
- **Balancing automation and personalization**: By incorporating personalization elements into automated campaigns, marketers can create more personalized messaging that resonates with their audience.
- **Implementing data quality control**: Regularly reviewing and cleaning data can help to ensure accuracy and relevancy in targeting.

Finding the right balance of automation: Finding the right balance between automation and manual control can help to ensure campaigns remain relevant and effective.

In summary, by taking these steps, affiliate marketers can overcome common challenges and ensure their automation efforts lead to successful campaigns.

Chapter 8

Conclusion

8.1 Recap of the key takeaways from the book

Here is a recap of the key takeaways from the book on affiliate marketing automation:

> - Affiliate marketing automation involves using tools and technologies to streamline and automate various tasks and processes in your affiliate marketing campaigns.

> - Automation can save time, improve efficiency, and help you scale your affiliate marketing efforts.

> - Common automation tools and technologies used in affiliate marketing include autoresponders, CRM systems, analytics software, and affiliate tracking software.

> - Advantages of automation include increased productivity, improved accuracy, and the ability to process large amounts of data quickly.

> - Disadvantages of automation include the cost of implementing and maintaining automated systems, potential errors or glitches, and the risk of losing the personal touch in your marketing efforts.

To create an effective automated system, it is important to identify your goals and objectives, determine which tasks can be automated, choose the right tools, and analyze and measure your campaign's performance.

Testing and refining your automated campaigns is important to ensure they are working effectively and producing the desired results.

Challenges faced in affiliate marketing automation include data management, system integration, and maintaining a human touch.

Strategies for overcoming these challenges include investing in training, staying up-to-date with the latest automation tools and technologies, and focusing on building relationships with customers and partners.

Tools and resources for scaling your affiliate marketing automation efforts include software and tools for data analysis, content creation, and customer relationship management.

8.2 Final thoughts on the importance of affiliate marketing automation

In conclusion, affiliate marketing automation can greatly improve the efficiency and effectiveness of your affiliate marketing campaigns. It allows you to streamline your workflow, save time and resources, and reach a wider audience. By automating repetitive tasks, you can focus on

more strategic aspects of your campaigns such as developing high-quality content and building relationships with your audience and partners.

However, it is important to remember that automation is not a one-size-fits-all solution and requires careful planning, implementation, and monitoring to achieve success.

Choosing the right tools and technologies, identifying your goals and objectives, and testing and refining your campaigns are all critical components of a successful automated system.

Ultimately, by investing in affiliate marketing automation, you can maximize your earning potential and achieve long-term success in the competitive world of affiliate marketing.

8.3 Resources and tools for further learning and growth in affiliate marketing automation.

Here are some resources and tools for further learning and growth in affiliate marketing automation:

AffTrack - A popular affiliate marketing tracking platform that allows you to automate your campaigns and track your performance.

HasOffers - An affiliate marketing software platform that provides tools for managing and tracking affiliate campaigns.

Voluum - A real-time analytics and optimization platform for affiliate marketers that helps automate their campaigns.

Zapier - A powerful automation tool that connects different apps and services, allowing you to automate tasks and workflows.

Click Funnels - A popular funnel builder that allows you to automate your sales funnel and create landing pages for your affiliate campaigns.

HubSpot - A comprehensive marketing automation tool that allows you to create email campaigns, automate your social media posts, and track your performance.

Udemy - An online learning platform that offers courses on affiliate marketing automation and other related topics.

Affiliate Summit - An annual conference that brings together affiliate marketers and industry experts to discuss the latest trends and best practices in the industry.

Affiliate Marketing Mastery - A comprehensive training program created by affiliate marketing expert Stefan James that teaches you how to build a successful affiliate marketing business, including automation strategies.

Digital Marketer - A digital marketing blog and training platform that offers courses on automation and other related topics.

By using these resources and tools, you can continue to learn and grow in your affiliate marketing automation efforts, and stay on top of the latest trends and strategies in the industry.

High-Ticket Affiliate Marketing:

Strategies for promoting high-value products and services and earning large commissions.

Chapter 1

Introduction

In today's digital age, affiliate marketing has become one of the most popular ways for people to earn income online. Whether you're a blogger, social media influencer, or just someone looking to make some extra money on the side, affiliate marketing provides a flexible and low-risk way to earn commissions by promoting other people's products and services.

While traditional affiliate marketing typically involves promoting low-priced products with lower commissions, high-ticket affiliate marketing offers the potential for much larger payouts.

High-ticket affiliate marketing involves promoting products and services that are more expensive, but also provide greater value and benefits to customers. This can include anything from luxury travel packages to high-end coaching programs and software solutions.

By focusing on high-ticket affiliate marketing, you can earn larger commissions for each sale you make, potentially earning thousands of dollars per sale rather than just a few dollars.

However, high-ticket affiliate marketing requires a different approach and set of strategies compared to traditional affiliate marketing. To be successful in this space, you'll need to understand the unique challenges and opportunities of promoting high-ticket offers, and develop a tailored marketing strategy that effectively reaches your target audience and persuades them to make a purchase.

In this book, we'll guide you through the ins and outs of high-ticket affiliate marketing, covering everything from identifying high-ticket affiliate offers to creating effective marketing campaigns that maximize your earnings potential. We'll provide you with practical advice, real-world examples, and actionable tips to help you succeed in this exciting and lucrative field. So whether you're a seasoned affiliate marketer or just getting started, this book is your comprehensive guide to succeeding in high-ticket affiliate marketing.

Affiliate marketing is a rapidly growing industry, with more and more people turning to it as a way to make money online. According to a recent survey, affiliate marketing spending in the US is expected to reach $8.2 billion by 2022, highlighting the immense potential of this field.

However, while there are plenty of low-ticket affiliate marketing opportunities available, the real money lies in high-ticket affiliate marketing. With high-ticket affiliate marketing, you have the potential to earn large commissions from a single sale, allowing you to earn more while putting in less work.

The key to succeeding in high-ticket affiliate marketing lies in understanding the unique challenges and opportunities of promoting high-ticket products and services. Unlike lower-priced products, high-ticket products require a different approach to marketing, with a greater focus on building trust and establishing credibility with potential customers.

In this book, we'll show you how to identify high-ticket affiliate offers, develop a tailored marketing strategy that effectively reaches your target audience, and create compelling marketing campaigns that maximize your earnings potential.

We'll cover topics such as:

The difference between traditional affiliate marketing and high-ticket affiliate marketing.

How to find high-ticket affiliate offers in different niches and industries

Strategies for building a strong brand and online presence to establish credibility and trust with your audience.

Creating effective sales copy and marketing materials that resonate with your target audience.

Techniques for overcoming objections and convincing prospects to make high-ticket purchases.

Tips for optimizing your sales funnel and maximizing conversions.

By the end of this book, you'll have a clear understanding of what it takes to succeed in high-ticket affiliate marketing, and the practical skills and

knowledge needed to start earning large commissions from your promotional efforts. Whether you're a seasoned affiliate marketer or just getting started, this book is your ultimate guide to succeeding in high-ticket affiliate marketing.

1.1 Explanation of high-ticket affiliate marketing and its potential for generating substantial commissions

High-ticket affiliate marketing refers to the practice of promoting expensive products or services and earning large commissions on each sale. Typically, high-ticket items have a price point of $1,000 or more, and can include things like luxury travel packages, high-end coaching programs, software solutions, and more.

Unlike traditional affiliate marketing, which focuses on promoting low-priced items with lower commissions, high-ticket affiliate marketing offers the potential for much larger payouts. With commissions ranging from 20% to 50% or more, high-ticket affiliate marketing has the potential to generate substantial income for those who are successful.

One of the main advantages of high-ticket affiliate marketing is that you don't need to make as many sales to generate significant income. While low-ticket affiliate marketing may require you to make hundreds or even thousands of sales to earn a decent income, with high-ticket affiliate

marketing, you can earn the same amount of money from just a handful of sales.

Additionally, high-ticket items are often associated with higher perceived value and greater benefits to customers. This means that they can be easier to promote to the right audience, as people are often willing to spend more money on products or services that offer a greater return on investment.

However, promoting high-ticket items also requires a different approach compared to promoting lower-priced products. You'll need to establish credibility and trust with your audience, and develop a marketing strategy that effectively reaches your target audience and persuades them to make a purchase.

With the right strategies and techniques, high-ticket affiliate marketing has the potential to generate substantial income and create a reliable source of passive income. So, if you're looking to take your affiliate marketing efforts to the next level, consider exploring the opportunities available in high-ticket affiliate marketing.

High-ticket affiliate marketing has gained popularity in recent years as more and more companies and entrepreneurs have begun to recognize the potential for generating significant income from promoting high-ticket items. In addition to the potential for higher commissions, high-ticket affiliate marketing also allows affiliates to focus on promoting products

and services that align with their interests and values, which can lead to greater job satisfaction and a more rewarding career.

One of the key advantages of high-ticket affiliate marketing is that it can offer a more stable source of income compared to traditional affiliate marketing. With lower-priced products, commissions can be small, and sales can fluctuate greatly depending on factors like seasonality, marketing trends, and consumer behavior. High-ticket items, on the other hand, tend to be more evergreen, with a longer sales cycle and a more stable customer base.

Another advantage of high-ticket affiliate marketing is that it allows affiliates to focus on building relationships with their audience, rather than just making quick sales. By developing a strong brand and online presence, and establishing themselves as experts in their niche, affiliates can build trust and credibility with their audience, leading to higher conversion rates and a greater likelihood of repeat sales.

However, it's important to note that high-ticket affiliate marketing does require more effort and skill compared to traditional affiliate marketing. Affiliates must be able to identify the right high-ticket products and services to promote, and develop a tailored marketing strategy that effectively reaches their target audience.

They must also be able to create compelling marketing materials, such as sales copy, videos, and social media posts that effectively communicate the value of the products or services they are promoting.

And, they must be able to provide excellent customer service and support, to ensure that customers are satisfied with their purchase and are more likely to make additional purchases in the future.

In summary, high-ticket affiliate marketing has the potential to generate substantial income and create a more rewarding and fulfilling career for those who are willing to put in the time and effort required. By understanding the unique challenges and opportunities of promoting high-ticket items, and developing a tailored marketing strategy that effectively reaches your target audience, you can position yourself for success in this exciting and lucrative field.

Chapter 2

Understanding High-Ticket Affiliate Marketing

High-ticket affiliate marketing refers to the practice of promoting expensive products or services as an affiliate marketer and earning large commissions on each sale. These products typically have a price point of $1,000 or more and can include high-end coaching programs, luxury travel packages, software solutions, and more.

One of the key advantages of high-ticket affiliate marketing is that it allows affiliates to earn large commissions from just a few sales, compared to traditional affiliate marketing, where you may need to make hundreds or thousands of sales to earn a decent income. Additionally, high-ticket items are often associated with higher perceived value and greater benefits to customers, making them more attractive to promote.

To succeed in high-ticket affiliate marketing, affiliates must identify the right products to promote and develop a tailored marketing strategy that effectively reaches their target audience. This often involves building a strong online presence, establishing credibility and trust with your audience, and developing compelling marketing materials that effectively communicate the value of the products or services you are promoting.

One of the challenges of high-ticket affiliate marketing is that it requires more effort and skill than traditional affiliate marketing. Affiliates must

be able to provide excellent customer service and support, to ensure that customers are satisfied with their purchase and are more likely to make additional purchases in the future.

Overall, high-ticket affiliate marketing offers the potential for significant income and a more rewarding and fulfilling career for those who are willing to put in the time and effort required. By understanding the unique challenges and opportunities of promoting high-ticket items, and developing a tailored marketing strategy that effectively reaches your target audience, you can position yourself for success in this exciting and lucrative field.

2.1 Concept of high-ticket products and services

High-ticket products and services refer to items that have a high price point, typically above $1,000, and offer significant value to the customer. These can include luxury goods, high-end services, advanced software solutions, and more.

The key feature of high-ticket products and services is that they offer a premium level of quality, exclusivity, and performance. They often provide unique features, superior materials, and advanced functionality that cannot be found in cheaper alternatives. As a result, high-ticket

items are associated with higher perceived value, greater benefits, and a more satisfying experience for the customer.

One advantage of high-ticket products and services is that they allow businesses to offer more personalized and customized solutions that meet the specific needs and preferences of their customers. For example, a luxury car manufacturer may offer customized options for the interior, exterior, and performance of the vehicle, providing a unique and personalized driving experience.

Another advantage of high-ticket products and services is that they can create a sense of exclusivity and prestige for customers. Many people are willing to pay a premium price for products and services that are perceived as exclusive or elite, and that provide a sense of social status or accomplishment.

However, it's important to note that high-ticket products and services are not for everyone. They require a significant investment of money and are often targeted towards a niche market with specific needs and preferences. As a result, businesses must have a clear understanding of their target audience and their unique selling proposition to effectively market and sell high-ticket items.

2.2 Comparison of high-ticket affiliate marketing to traditional affiliate marketing

When it comes to affiliate marketing, there are two main approaches: traditional affiliate marketing and high-ticket affiliate marketing. Traditional affiliate marketing typically involves promoting lower-priced products or services, while high-ticket affiliate marketing focuses on promoting higher-priced products or services.

One of the main differences between these two approaches is the commission structure. With traditional affiliate marketing, commissions are typically lower, ranging from 5% to 30% of the sale price. In contrast, high-ticket affiliate marketing often offers higher commission rates, ranging from 30% to 50% or more of the sale price. This means that affiliates can earn substantially more money per sale with high-ticket items.

Another difference is the level of competition. Traditional affiliate marketing tends to be more competitive, as there are often many affiliates promoting the same products or services. This can make it more difficult to stand out and earn commissions. In contrast, high-ticket affiliate marketing typically has less competition, as there are fewer affiliates promoting these higher-priced items.

However, promoting high-ticket items can be more challenging and require a greater investment of time, effort, and resources. This is because high-ticket items often require a more targeted and customized marketing approach, and may require more education and research to effectively promote. Additionally, promoting high-ticket items may require a greater investment of money in paid advertising and other promotional methods.

It's also important to note that the target audience for high-ticket items may be smaller than for lower-priced items. This means that affiliates need to have a clear understanding of their niche market and target audience to effectively promote high-ticket items.

In summary, high-ticket affiliate marketing offers the potential for greater earnings and less competition compared to traditional affiliate marketing. However, it also requires a greater investment of time, effort, and resources, as well as a targeted and customized marketing approach. Affiliates must carefully evaluate their goals, niche market, and target audience to determine whether high-ticket affiliate marketing is the right approach for them.

2.3 Advantages and disadvantages of promoting high-ticket offers

Promoting high-ticket offers can offer both advantages and disadvantages to affiliate marketers. Here are some of the key pros and cons to consider:

Advantages:

- **Higher commission rates**: High-ticket offers typically offer higher commission rates than lower-priced offers. This means that affiliates can earn more money per sale, which can result in greater profits and a higher income.

- **Targeted audience**: High-ticket offers are often targeted to a specific audience, such as those who are looking for luxury products or high-end services. This means that affiliates can focus their marketing efforts on a specific niche and attract high-quality leads who are more likely to convert into customers.

- **Greater perceived value**: High-ticket offers often have a greater perceived value than lower-priced offers. This means that customers are willing to pay more for these products or services, which can lead to higher conversion rates and more sales.

Disadvantages:

- **Higher investment**: Promoting high-ticket offers often requires a greater investment of time, effort, and resources. Affiliates may need to create custom landing pages, invest in paid advertising, or conduct extensive market research to effectively promote these offers.

- **Smaller audience**: High-ticket offers are often targeted to a specific audience, which means that the potential customer base may be smaller than for lower-priced offers. This can make it more difficult to generate traffic and leads.

- **Greater competition**: While there may be less competition in the high-ticket niche overall, there may be greater competition for specific high-ticket offers. This means that affiliates may need to work harder to differentiate themselves from other affiliates promoting the same offers.

In summary, promoting high-ticket offers can offer higher commission rates, a targeted audience, and greater perceived value. However, it may require a greater investment of time and resources and may have a smaller potential customer base and greater competition. Affiliates should carefully consider their goals and resources when deciding whether to promote high-ticket offers.

Chapter 3

Identifying High-Ticket Affiliate Offers

3.1 How to find high-ticket affiliate offers in different niches

Finding high-ticket affiliate offers in different niches can be a challenging task, but there are several strategies that affiliates can use to identify potential opportunities:

- **Search affiliate networks**: Many affiliate networks, such as ShareASale, CJ Affiliate, and Clickbank, have a wide variety of high-ticket offers in different niches. Affiliates can search for offers based on their niche, commission rate, and other criteria to find potential opportunities.

- **Research product and service providers**: Affiliates can research different product and service providers in their niche to identify high-ticket offers. This may involve researching different companies and brands, reading industry publications and blogs, and attending industry events and conferences.

- **Follow industry influencers**: Following influencers and thought leaders in your niche can help you identify high-ticket affiliate offers. These individuals may have partnerships with companies and brands that offer high-ticket products or services and may promote these offers on their blogs or social media channels.

- **Join private affiliate programs**: Some companies may have private affiliate programs that offer high commission rates for their products or services. These programs may not be listed on affiliate networks, so affiliates can contact companies directly to inquire about their affiliate programs.

- **Attend webinars and training sessions**: Many companies and brands offer webinars and training sessions to help their affiliates promote their products or services effectively.

Attending these sessions can help affiliates identify high-ticket offers and learn about the best ways to promote them.

In summary, affiliates can use a variety of strategies to find high-ticket affiliate offers in different niches. By researching affiliate networks, product and service providers, industry influencers, private affiliate programs, and attending webinars and training sessions, affiliates can identify potential opportunities and earn higher commissions on their sales.

3.2 Criteria for evaluating the potential profitability of high-ticket offers

Evaluating the potential profitability of high-ticket offers is essential for affiliate marketers to determine whether a particular offer is worth promoting. Here are some criteria to consider when assessing the potential profitability of high-ticket offers:

- **Commission rate**: The commission rate is a key factor in determining the profitability of a high-ticket offer. The higher the commission rate, the more money affiliates can earn per sale.

- **Conversion rate**: The conversion rate refers to the percentage of leads that convert into customers. A high conversion rate means that more leads are likely to purchase the high-ticket offer, which can increase the profitability of the promotion.

- **Average order value (AOV)**: AOV refers to the average amount of money that customers spend on a single purchase. High-ticket offers typically have a higher AOV, which means that affiliates can earn more money per sale.

- **Affiliate resources**: The availability of resources, such as marketing materials, landing pages, and support from the product or service provider, can impact the profitability of a high-ticket offer. The more resources that are available, the easier it may be to promote the offer and attract leads.

- **Target audience**: The target audience for the high-ticket offer can also impact its profitability. A well-defined target audience with a high propensity to purchase high-ticket products or services can increase the likelihood of sales and profits.

- **Competition**: The level of competition in the niche or industry can also impact the profitability of the offer. The more competition there is, the harder it may be to attract leads and make sales.

In summary, evaluating the potential profitability of high-ticket offers involves considering the commission rate, conversion rate, AOV, available resources, target audience, and competition. By carefully assessing these factors, affiliate marketers can identify the most profitable high-ticket offers to promote and maximize their earnings.

3.3 Examples of high-ticket affiliate programs and offers

Here are some examples of high-ticket affiliate programs and offers in various niches:

- **Health and wellness**: Some health and wellness companies offer high-ticket programs, such as weight loss coaching or specialized diets. For example, the WildFit program by Mindvalley offers a 35% commission on a $1,000 program that teaches healthy eating habits and nutrition.

- **Business and finance**: Some financial and business coaching programs offer high-ticket commissions for affiliates. For example, Tony Robbins' Business Mastery program offers affiliates up to $3,000 in commissions for promoting a $10,000 event ticket.

- **Technology**: High-ticket technology products, such as web development services or marketing automation software, can offer high commissions for affiliates. For example, HubSpot offers a 20% commission on their Marketing Hub and Sales Hub products, which can range from $9,600 to $38,400 per year.

- **Travel**: High-end travel and vacation packages can also offer high commissions for affiliates. For example, Sandals Resorts offers a 4% commission on all bookings, which can range from a few thousand dollars to tens of thousands of dollars for luxury vacation packages.

- **Education**: Some educational programs, such as online courses or certifications, can offer high-ticket commissions for affiliates. For example, the DigitalMarketer Certified Partner Program offers a 30% commission on a $5,000 certification program.

These are just a few examples of high-ticket affiliate programs and offers in various niches. As mentioned earlier, affiliates can search for high-ticket offers on affiliate networks, research product and service providers, follow industry influencers, and attend webinars and training sessions to identify potential opportunities.

Chapter 4

Creating a High-Ticket Affiliate Marketing Strategy

4.1 How to define your target audience and their pain points

Defining your target audience and understanding their pain points is critical for creating an effective high-ticket affiliate marketing strategy. Here are some steps to help you define your target audience and identify their pain points:

- **Conduct market research**: Start by researching your niche or industry to understand the needs and preferences of your target audience. This can involve analyzing competitors, conducting surveys, and gathering feedback from potential customers.

- **Create customer personas**: Based on your research, create customer personas that represent the different types of people who might be interested in your high-ticket offer.

Each persona should include demographic information, such as age, gender, and location, as well as psychographic information, such as interests, values, and motivations.

- **Identify pain points**: Once you have created customer personas, identify their pain points or challenges. This can involve conducting surveys or interviews to understand the specific problems your target audience is facing and the solutions they are looking for.

- **Develop a value proposition**: Based on the pain points you have identified, develop a value proposition that highlights the benefits of your high-ticket offer and how it addresses your target audience's pain points. This value proposition should be clear and concise, and communicate why your high-ticket offer is better than other solutions in the market.

- **Refine your message**: Once you have developed a value proposition, refine your messaging to ensure that it resonates with your target audience. This can involve testing different headlines, copy, and visual elements to see what works best.

- **Monitor and adjust**: Finally, monitor your marketing efforts and adjust your strategy as needed. Pay attention to the feedback you receive from your target audience and make changes to your messaging and positioning to better address their pain points.

By following these steps, you can define your target audience, understand their pain points, and develop a high-ticket affiliate marketing strategy that resonates with them and drives conversions.

4.2 Develop a content strategy to attract and engage your audience

Developing a content strategy is essential to attract and engage your target audience and promote your high-ticket affiliate offer effectively. Here are some steps to help you develop a content strategy for your high-ticket affiliate marketing campaign:

- **Identify your target audience**: Start by identifying your target audience and understanding their needs and preferences. This will help you create content that resonates with them and addresses their pain points.

- **Define your goals**: Determine the goals of your content strategy, such as increasing traffic, generating leads, or building brand awareness.

- **Choose your content types**: Decide which types of content you want to create, such as blog posts, videos, social media posts, webinars, or podcasts.

- **Create a content calendar**: Plan out your content in advance using a content calendar.

This should include topics, keywords, and publishing dates.

- **Use SEO best practices**: Incorporate SEO best practices, such as using relevant keywords, optimizing titles and meta descriptions, and including internal and external links.

- **Promote your content**: Use social media, email marketing, and other channels to promote your content and drive traffic to your website.

- **Measure your results**: Track your content performance using analytics tools to determine what is working and what needs to be adjusted.

- **Adjust your strategy**: Based on your results, adjust your content strategy and continue to optimize it over time.

By following these steps, you can create a content strategy that attracts and engages your target audience, promotes your high-ticket affiliate offer, and drives conversions.

4.3 Choosing the right marketing channels to promote your high-ticket offers

Choosing the right marketing channels is critical to effectively promote your high-ticket offers and reach your target audience. Here are some factors to consider when choosing marketing channels for your high-ticket affiliate marketing campaign:

Audience demographics: Consider the demographics of your target audience, such as age, gender, and location, to determine which marketing channels they are most likely to use. For example, if your target audience

is primarily young adults, social media channels like Instagram and Snapchat may be more effective than traditional marketing channels.

- **Budget**: Consider your budget when choosing marketing channels, as some channels may be more expensive than others. For example, paid advertising on social media or search engines can be costly, whereas email marketing and content marketing can be more budget-friendly.

- **Conversion rates**: Evaluate the conversion rates of different marketing channels to determine which ones are most effective at driving conversions. For example, email marketing may have a higher conversion rate than social media marketing.

- **Competition**: Consider the level of competition on different marketing channels to determine how easy it will be to stand out and reach your target audience. For example, social media channels like Facebook and Twitter may be highly competitive, whereas niche forums or industry-specific websites may be less crowded.

- **Brand messaging**: Consider how well different marketing channels align with your brand messaging and target audience. For example, if your high-ticket offer is geared towards a professional audience, LinkedIn may be a more effective marketing channel than Instagram.

- **Analytics and data**: Use analytics tools and data to evaluate the performance of different marketing channels and adjust your strategy accordingly. For example, if your website analytics show that most of your traffic is coming from search engines, it may be beneficial to invest in search engine optimization (SEO).

By considering these factors, you can choose the marketing channels that are most likely to reach your target audience, drive conversions, and maximize the ROI of your high-ticket affiliate marketing campaign.

4.4. Building a strong brand and online presence to establish credibility and trust

Building a strong brand and online presence is crucial to establish credibility and trust with your target audience. Here are some steps you can take to build a strong brand and online presence for your high-ticket affiliate marketing campaign:

- **Define your brand identity**: Start by defining your brand identity, including your brand values, mission, and tone of voice. This will help you create a consistent brand image across all marketing channels.

- **Create a professional website**: Invest in a professional website that reflects your brand identity and offers a positive user experience. Ensure that your website is mobile-responsive, easy to navigate, and optimized for search engines.

- **Use consistent branding**: Use consistent branding across all marketing channels, including your website, social media, email marketing, and advertising. This includes using consistent colors, fonts, and imagery.

- **Engage with your audience**: Engage with your target audience through social media, email marketing, and other channels. Respond to comments and messages promptly and provide valuable content and resources to establish trust and credibility.

- **Build a strong social media presence**: Use social media platforms to build a strong online presence and engage with your target audience. Choose the platforms that align with your target audience and use them to share valuable content, promote your high-ticket offers, and build relationships.

- **Leverage influencer marketing**: Partner with influencers in your niche to promote your high-ticket offers and build credibility with your target audience.

- **Use customer testimonials and reviews**: Use customer testimonials and reviews on your website and other marketing channels to build social proof and establish credibility.

By following these steps, you can build a strong brand and online presence that establishes credibility and trust with your target audience, and increases the likelihood of driving conversions for your high-ticket affiliate offers.

Chapter 5

Effective Promotion and Conversion Tactics

5.1 How to create effective sales copy and marketing materials to promote high-ticket offers

Creating effective sales copy and marketing materials is essential for promoting high-ticket offers. Here are some tips to help you create compelling sales copy and marketing materials:

- **Understand your target audience**: Before you start creating sales copy and marketing materials, you need to understand your target audience and their pain points. Use this information to craft messaging that resonates with them.

- **Highlight the benefits**: Focus on the benefits of the high-ticket offer you are promoting, rather than just the features. Clearly explain how the product or service can solve your target audience's pain points and improve their lives.

- **Use persuasive language**: Use persuasive language to encourage your target audience to take action. This includes using power words, emotional triggers, and compelling calls to action.

- **Create a sense of urgency**: Create a sense of urgency by emphasizing limited-time offers, scarcity, and exclusivity. This can help to motivate your target audience to take action and make a purchase.

- **Use social proof**: Use social proof, such as customer testimonials and case studies, to demonstrate the effectiveness of the high-ticket offer you are promoting. This can help to build credibility and trust with your target audience.

- **Use visuals**: Incorporate visuals, such as images and videos, to make your sales copy and marketing materials more engaging and memorable.

- **Keep it simple**: Keep your sales copy and marketing materials simple and easy to understand. Avoid using technical jargon or complicated language that could confuse or alienate your target audience.

By following these tips, you can create effective sales copy and marketing materials that effectively promote your high-ticket offers and drive conversions.

5.2 Implementing strategies for pre-selling and warming up leads before promoting high-ticket offers

Implementing pre-selling and lead warming strategies is a critical part of promoting high-ticket offers. Here are some strategies that you can use:

- **Content marketing**: Create valuable content that educates your target audience about the problem your high-ticket offer solves. Use blog posts, videos, social media posts, and email newsletters to build a relationship with your audience and establish yourself as an authority in your niche.

- **Email marketing**: Use email marketing to nurture leads and build a relationship with them before promoting your high-ticket offer. Send out a series of emails that educate and inform your leads about the problem your offer solves and how it can help them.

- **Webinars**: Host webinars that educate your target audience about the problem your high-ticket offer solves and demonstrate the value of your offer. Use the webinar to build a relationship with your audience and answer their questions.

- **Case studies**: Share case studies of customers who have successfully used your high-ticket offer to solve their problems. This can help to build trust and credibility with your target audience.

- **Free trials or consultations**: Offer free trials or consultations to help your target audience experience the value of your high-ticket offer. This can help to overcome objections and build trust with your audience.

By implementing these strategies, you can pre-sell and warm up your leads before promoting your high-ticket offer. This can help to build trust, overcome objections, and increase the likelihood of driving conversions for your high-ticket affiliate offers.

5.3 Techniques for overcoming objections and convincing prospects to make high-ticket purchases

Overcoming objections and convincing prospects to make high-ticket purchases is essential for driving conversions. Here are some techniques that can help you overcome objections and close the sale:

- **Understand the objection**: Before you can overcome an objection, you need to understand what the objection is. Ask your prospect to explain their objection in detail and listen carefully to their response.

- **Address the objection**: Once you understand the objection, address it directly. Provide a solution or explanation

5.4 Tips for optimizing your sales funnel and maximizing conversions

Optimizing your sales funnel is essential for maximizing conversions and driving revenue. Here are some tips for optimizing your sales funnel:

- **Understand your audience**: Understanding your audience is key to creating a sales funnel that resonates with them. Research your target audience's pain points, needs, and behaviors to create a funnel that addresses their specific needs.
- **Create a clear and compelling value proposition**: Your value proposition should clearly explain how your high-ticket offer solves your audience's problems and why it's worth the investment.
- **Use high-converting landing pages**: Your landing pages should be optimized for conversion. Use clear and compelling copy, visually appealing design, and a strong call-to-action to encourage conversions.

- **Use retargeting ads**: Retargeting ads can help you re-engage prospects who have shown interest in your high-ticket offer but haven't yet converted. Use retargeting ads to remind prospects about the value of your offer and encourage them to take action.

- **Offer incentives**: Incentives such as discounts, bonuses, or free trials can help to overcome objections and encourage prospects to make a purchase.
- **Test and optimize**: Continuously test and optimize your sales funnel to identify areas for improvement and maximize conversions. Use A/B testing to compare different versions of your landing pages and marketing materials to see which ones perform best.

By following these tips, you can optimize your sales funnel and maximize conversions for your high-ticket affiliate offers.

Chapter 6

Maximizing Your High-Ticket Affiliate Marketing Results

6.1 How to track and analyze your affiliate marketing results

Tracking and analyzing your affiliate marketing results is essential for understanding your performance and identifying areas for improvement. Here are some steps you can take to track and analyze your results:

- **Set up tracking links**: Tracking links allow you to track the performance of your affiliate marketing campaigns. Use a tool such as Google Analytics or a dedicated affiliate tracking software to set up tracking links for each of your campaigns.

- **Monitor key metrics**: Key metrics to monitor include clicks, impressions, conversions, conversion rate, and revenue. Use your tracking software to monitor these metrics and identify trends over time.

- **Analyze your audience**: Use the data from your tracking software to analyze your audience. Identify demographic information, such as age and gender, as well as behavioral data, such as interests and purchasing habits.

- **Identify top-performing campaigns**: Analyze your data to identify your top-performing campaigns. Look for patterns and insights that can help you replicate success in future campaigns.

- **Make data-driven decisions**: Use the insights from your data analysis to make data-driven decisions about your affiliate marketing strategy. Use the data to optimize your campaigns, improve targeting, and increase conversions.

By tracking and analyzing your affiliate marketing results, you can gain valuable insights into your performance and make data-driven decisions to improve your results over time.

6.2 Strategies for scaling your high-ticket affiliate marketing efforts and earning even larger commissions

Scaling your high-ticket affiliate marketing efforts can help you earn even larger commissions and grow your business. Here are some strategies for scaling your high-ticket affiliate marketing efforts:

- **Expand your audience**: Expanding your audience can help you reach more potential customers and increase your conversions. Look for opportunities to reach new audiences through targeted advertising, social media marketing, and other channels.

- **Diversify your campaigns**: Diversifying your campaigns can help you reach different segments of your audience and increase your overall revenue. Look for opportunities to promote different high-ticket affiliate offers to your audience.

- **Build relationships with merchants**: Building strong relationships with merchants can help you secure exclusive offers and access to new high-ticket products or services. Work with your merchant partners to identify opportunities for collaboration and promotion.

- **Use automation tools**: Using automation tools can help you streamline your workflow and save time on repetitive tasks. Look for opportunities to automate your lead generation, email marketing, and other marketing activities.

- **Create passive income streams**: Creating passive income streams can help you earn commissions even when you're not actively promoting a high-ticket offer. Look for opportunities to create evergreen content or promote recurring subscription services.

By implementing these strategies, you can scale your high-ticket affiliate marketing efforts and earn even larger commissions over time. Remember to always focus on providing value to your audience and building strong relationships with your merchant partners.

6.3 Tools and resources for streamlining your high-ticket affiliate marketing workflow

Streamlining your high-ticket affiliate marketing workflow can help you save time and increase your productivity. Here are some tools and resources that can help you streamline your workflow:

- **Affiliate tracking software**: Affiliate tracking software can help you manage your campaigns and track your performance. Look for a software that provides real-time reporting and analytics, as well as advanced features such as split testing and conversion optimization.

- **Content management systems**: Content management systems (CMS) can help you manage your website and create content more efficiently. Look for a CMS that is user-friendly and customizable, and that integrates with your affiliate tracking software.

- **Email marketing software**: Email marketing software can help you automate your email campaigns and build relationships with your subscribers. Look for a software that provides customizable templates, automated workflows, and advanced segmentation features.

- **Social media management tools**: Social media management tools can help you manage your social media accounts more efficiently.

  Look for a tool that provides scheduling, analytics, and engagement features, as well as integrations with other marketing software.

- **Outsourcing services**: Outsourcing services can help you delegate tasks and free up your time for higher-value activities. Look for a reputable outsourcing service that provides high-quality work at a reasonable cost.

By using these tools and resources, you can streamline your high-ticket affiliate marketing workflow and focus on the activities that generate the most revenue for your business. Remember to always prioritize providing value to your audience and building strong relationships with your merchant partners.

Chapter 7

Conclusion

7.1 Summary of key takeaways from the book

Here are the key takeaways from the book on high-ticket affiliate marketing:

- High-ticket affiliate marketing is a lucrative opportunity that involves promoting high-value products and services that generate substantial commissions.

- To succeed in high-ticket affiliate marketing, you need to define your target audience and their pain points, and develop a content strategy to attract and engage them.

- You should focus on promoting high-ticket offers that have a high potential for profitability, based on criteria such as commission rates, conversion rates, and demand.

- Building a strong brand and online presence is essential for establishing credibility and trust with your audience, and optimizing your sales funnel can help maximize conversions.

- Overcoming objections and convincing prospects to make high-ticket purchases requires effective sales copy, as well as pre-selling and warming up leads before promoting the offer.

- Tools and resources such as affiliate tracking software, content management systems, email marketing software, social media management tools, and outsourcing services can help streamline your workflow and increase your productivity.
- By following these key takeaways and applying the strategies and tips outlined in the book, you can achieve success in high-ticket affiliate marketing and earn substantial commissions.

7.2 Interviews with successful high-ticket affiliate marketers

Some successful high-ticket affiliate marketers are:

- Pat Flynn - Pat Flynn is a well-known affiliate marketer who has generated millions of dollars in commissions through his website, Smart Passive Income. He promotes high-ticket products such as courses and software, and focuses on building trust with his audience through valuable content and transparent marketing.
- John Crestani - John Crestani is an affiliate marketer who has earned millions of dollars promoting high-ticket offers in the internet marketing niche. He is known for his expertise in paid advertising, particularly through Facebook ads.
- Robby Blanchard - Robby Blanchard is a successful affiliate marketer who specializes in promoting high-ticket offers in the

fitness and health niches. He has generated millions of dollars in commissions by using Facbook ads and building email lists to promote his offers.

- Spencer Mecham - Spencer Mecham is an affiliate marketer who has generated over $1 million in commissions promoting high-ticket affiliate offers in the online marketing niche. He is known for his expertise in building sales funnels and creating valuable content to attract and convert leads.

These successful high-ticket affiliate marketers have different approaches and strategies, but they all focus on providing value to their audience, building trust and authority, and using targeted marketing tactics to promote high-ticket offers.

Made in the USA
Las Vegas, NV
29 April 2024

89296127R10079